MINDFUL MANTRA

I'M PROUD OF MYSELF!

My name is James and I am PROUD OF MYSELF!

By Laurie Wright
Illustrations by Ana Santos

I was feeling nervous about joining the next level of soccer team.

I had to learn new skills.

I had to keep up.

I had to practice over
and over.

Now I play much better.
I am proud of myself!

I was feeling frustrated about not being able to tie my shoes yet.

I had to make a lot
of knots.

I had to growl like
an angry guinea pig.

I had to keep trying even
when I wanted to give up.

Now I am able to tie
my shoes right MOST of the time.
I am proud of myself.

I was feeling self-conscious about doing a presentation in my class.

I had to force myself to
stand up at the front.
(I didn't run away!)

I had to explain
to the kids about
my idea.

I had to do it even though
I really didn't want to.

Now I have talked in front of my class.
I am proud of myself!

I was feeling sad yesterday.

I had to cry.

I had to let people
cuddle me a little,
even though I'm big.

I had to tell myself it
was okay to be sad.

Now I have made it through my sad day!
I am proud of myself.

I was feeling worried about doing laps in my swim class.

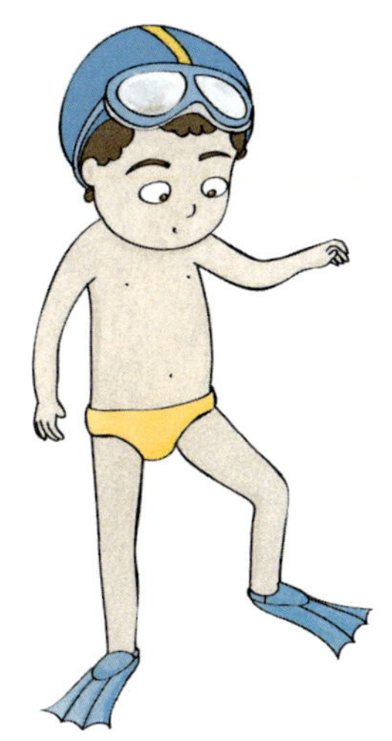

I had to give myself
a pep talk.

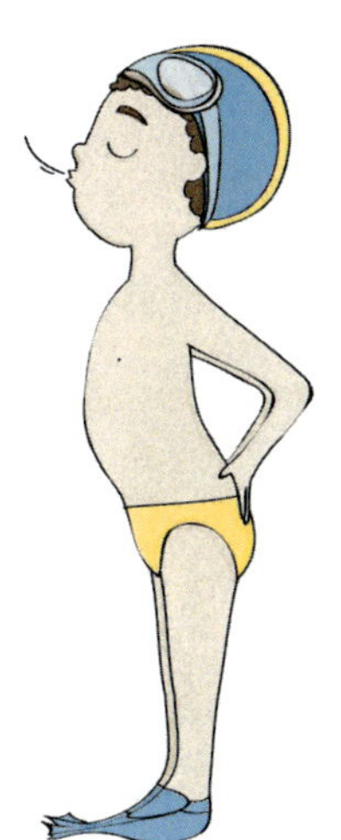

I had to take some deep
breaths to calm down.

I had to try really hard.

Now I have learned to swim laps!
I am proud of myself.

I was feeling angry when my little sister took the spot next to mom.

I had to sit alone
for a while.

I had to tell them how
I felt, without yelling.

I had to give her a turn
in the best spot.

Now I have handled
my sister taking my spot!
I am proud of myself.

I was feeling SO tired after a fun birthday sleepover.

I had to realize that
I was cranky and
being unkind.

I had to spend
some time alone.

I had to take a nap!

Now I have taken care of
myself when I was too tired.
I am proud of myself!

I was feeling shy at a summer camp when I didn't know anyone.

I had to smile at
a few people.

I had to say hi
to someone
I didn't know.

I had to take a chance.

Now I have made a new friend!
I am proud of myself.

I was feeling over-excited when I was going to get a new pet! (another guinea pig!)

I had to realize other
people weren't as excited
as I was.

I had to take some
deep breaths.

I had to go for a quick run
to get my energy out.

Now I've handled feeling
a little TOO excited.
I am proud of myself!

Sometimes I feel nervous, frustrated, self-conscious, sad, worried, angry, tired, shy or over-excited,

but I am always proud of myself!

My name is

____

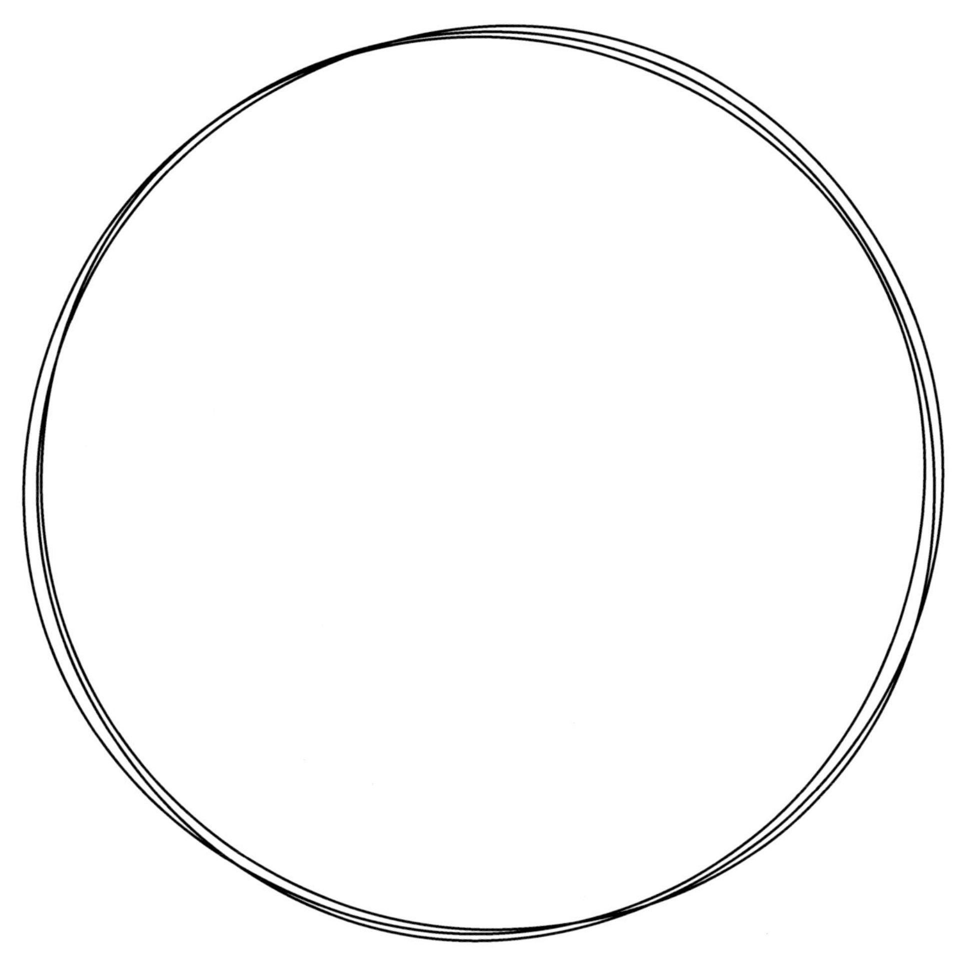

... and I am proud of myself!

Dear Reader,

After reading this book you've realized that it's important to be proud of yourself, even when things don't go as planned. Tell yourself every day that you are PROUD of what you've done even if things don't go as well as you'd expected.

I'd love to hear something that you are proud of yourself for, so send me an email and I'll write back to you for sure! (I promise!)

Now, let me ask you a question. Do you ever wonder if you'll be able to stay calm in a bad situation? Do you sometimes wonder if you might EXPLODE with anger or frustration? If you said YES to either of those, you will enjoy reading the book, "I Believe in Myself' in the Mindful Mantras series, which is about a girl named Poppy who isn't always sure she'll be able to control her emotions. I think it might help you to realize that other kids feel the same way you do.

You also might like a song to listen to that helps you remember that you should be proud of yourself! Ask an adult to sign up at lauriewrights.com/seven.

Finally, a great big THANK YOU for reading, I sincerely hope you enjoyed this book.

All my best,
Laurie Wright
*****

Laurie Wright

Laurie Wright is a speaker, author, and educator who is passionate about helping children increase their positive self-talk and improve their mental health. Laurie speaks to parents, teachers, and childcare providers, has given a TEDx talk, created resources and has written 7 books, all to further the cause of improving the self-esteem of our children. Laurie is a huge advocate for children's mental health and works every day to improve the way we interact with kids, and to help them learn to handle all of their emotions!

Ana Santos

Ana is a creative and innate illustrator and she feels very comfortable and inspired by all the challenges and areas that incorporate illustration and design. Graduated in graphic design, she dicovered her vocation for Arts as a child. Ana has already several years of experience in graphic design and illustration and she has already illustrated several edited children's books for people and publishers around the world! Ana is an artist attentive to new technologies working on many internet platforms as a freelancer.

Made in the USA
San Bernardino, CA
10 November 2018